W9-DFE-221

Machines Inside Machines

Using Springs

Wendy Sadler

Raintree

Chicago, Illinois

Printed and bound in China by South China Printing
Company

09 08 07 06 05
10 9 8 7 6 5 4 3 2 1

Library of Congress Cataloging-in-Publication Data:
Cataloging-in-Publication Data is on file at the Library
of Congress.

ISBN 1-4109-1446-1 (lib. binding), 1-4109-1453-4 (Pbk.)

Acknowledgments
The publishers would like to thank the following for
permission to reproduce photographs:
Alamy Images (Beateworks Inc) p. **15**; Alamy Images
(Ingram Publishing) p. **27**; Alamy Images (Leslie Garland
Picture Library) p. **19**; Corbis (George B.Diebold) p. **6**;
Corbis (H&S Produktion) p. **21**; Corbis (Kevin Fleming) p.
20; DK images p. **23**; Getty Images (Botanica) p. **5**;
Harcourt Education Ltd (Chrissie Martin) p. **18**; Harcourt
Education Ltd (Trevor Clifford) pp. **4, 17**; Harcourt
Education Ltd (Tudor Photography) pp. **7, 8, 9, 13, 14, 16,
22, 25, 26, 28, 29**; Peter Willis p. **10**; zefa/ masterfile (Gail
Mooney) p. **11**; zefa (Satchan) p. **12**.

Cover photograph of springs reproduced with permission
of Powerstock (SuperStock)

Disclaimer:
All the Internet addresses (URLs) given in this book were
valid at the time of going to press. However, due to the
dynamic nature of the Internet, some addresses may have
changed, or sites may have changed or ceased to exist since
publication. While the author and Publishers regret any
inconvenience this may cause readers, no responsibility
for any such changes can be accepted by either the author
or the Publishers.

Contents

Any words appearing in the text in bold,
like this, are explained in the glossary.

Machines That Use Springs

Springs are found in lots of different machines all around you. Springs can be squeezed together or stretched out. They can make things pop up or they can hold things in place. We sit on springs in sofas and chairs and sleep on springs in bed. Cars use springs to make your journey more comfortable. You might even use springs to keep your hair in place!

Springs in this garden chair make it more comfortable to sit on.

Springs are used in many machines. They can be useful for lots of jobs. They are usually used when you want to make something move or grip. Springs were used in old clocks to keep time. The most important thing about a spring is that it can store **energy.** Energy is the power to make things work. Springs are very simple, but very important.

The spring in these garden cutters helps push the blade apart after you have cut the plant.

What Is a Spring?

A spring is made of **material** wound into the shape of a **cylinder.** When material is wound in circles like this, it is called a **coil.** A spring needs to be made of **stiff** material to be useful. Springs are usually made of metal, but they can also be made of very strong plastic. Springs are useful because they naturally try to stay in their coil shape.

Metal is a stiff material that is good for making springs.

A **simple machine** is something that makes a job easier to do. A spring on its own is not a simple machine. Springs are often used with other simple machines such as wheels, **gears,** and **levers.** When several simple machines are used together, we call them **compound machines.** Springs are a very important part of lots of compound machines.

The spring in this umbrella holds the umbrella open until you are ready to close it.

What would happen without . . . ?

Without stiff material to make the spring hold its shape, the spring would not work. If you rolled some string into the shape of a spring, it would not try to hold its shape—it would just unravel.

How Does a Spring Work?

Springs like to always be in their usual shape—a **cylinder.** All **materials** are made up of tiny pieces called **particles.** The particles inside a spring have strong **forces** between them that hold the material together. When you stretch the spring out, you pull these particles apart. The particles want to get closer together again, so the spring pulls back into its original shape.

Some springs are made of strong material and are very difficult to stretch out. Other springs are made of weaker material and can be stretched out easily.

You can also squeeze a spring by pushing it together. This push makes the particles in the spring get very close together. The forces between them push the particles apart again, to try to return the spring to its usual shape. As soon as you let go, the spring jumps back into shape.

When you close the lid of this jack-in-a-box, you squeeze together the spring. When the lid opens, the spring stretches out again, and the toy on the end pops up!

Why Are Springs Useful?

Springs are useful because they let us store movement as **energy.** When you push or pull a spring, you use your energy to make it change shape. Your energy is now stored in the spring. When you let go, the spring uses the stored energy to move back into its original shape.

When this gate is open, the spring stretches out. As soon as you let go of the gate, the spring pulls back into shape and brings the gate with it.

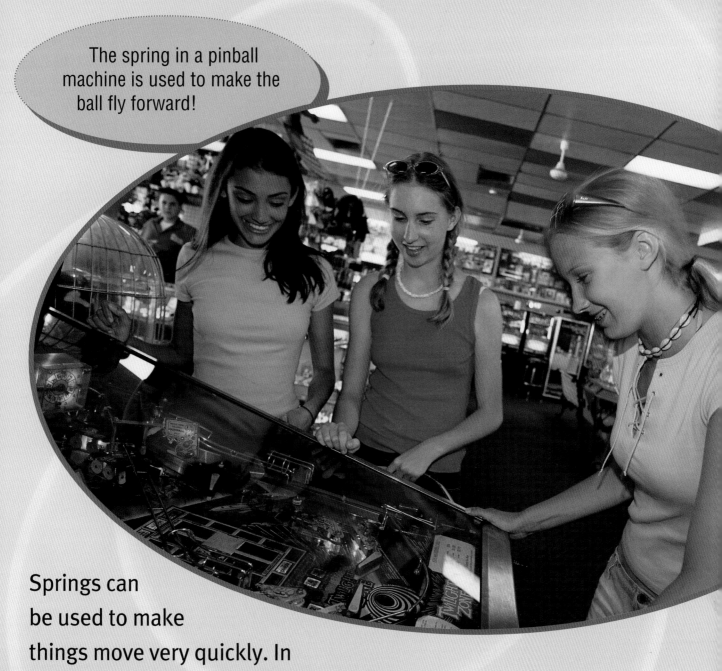

The spring in a pinball machine is used to make the ball fly forward!

Springs can be used to make things move very quickly. In a pinball machine, you have to try to shoot a ball at different targets to score points. To launch the ball, you pull the spring back so that it is squeezed together. The ball sits on the top of the spring. When you let the spring go, it jumps back into shape. The spring pushes the ball upward as it stretches out.

11

Different Types of Spring

An **expansion spring** is a spring that is made to be stretched out. The spring tries to pull itself back into shape. When an expansion spring is not stretched out, its **coils** are very close together—sometimes even touching each other.

This piece of exercise equipment is an expansion spring. This woman is using the strength in her arms to stretch the springs out.

Most springs can only be stretched out to a certain point. If the spring is stretched farther than this, the **particles** inside will slide past each other. The spring will lose its shape and stay stretched out. Once a spring has been stretched too far, it is very difficult to make it go back to its original shape.

Look at the shape of this spring. It has been stretched too far, and the coil shape has been changed. This spring will not go back to the shape that it was before.

13

Compression Springs

A **compression spring** is a spring that is used by squeezing it together to store **energy.** A compression spring needs to have some gaps between the **coils** when it is in its usual shape. If there were no gaps between the coils, the coils could not be pushed together.

Once a compression spring has been squeezed together so that all the coils are touching, it cannot be pushed any further.

spring

This hole punch uses compression springs. When you punch a hole, the springs squeeze together. When you let go, the springs push the hole punch apart again.

Compression springs can be used to grip things. Shower curtain rods can use these springs to hold them up. The spring inside the rod pushes out against the sides of the walls. This keeps the rod from falling down.

There is a compression spring inside this rod. It pushes against the wall to hold up the shower curtain rod.

Everyday Springs

Every time you switch on a light, you are possibly using a spring without knowing it! Some lights in your home may have strings attached to them. When you pull on the string, you squeeze together a spring inside the switch. When you let go of the string, the spring pushes the switch back upward. As the switch goes up, the light comes on.

There are springs all around your home—even in the closet light switch.

Pens can have springs inside them, too. If a pen does not have a lid, a spring switch can be used to push the writing end in and out of the pen.

Activity

1. Find a pen in your house that has a spring in the end. If you cannot see the spring, just try looking for any pen that has a push button on top.
2. Ask an adult to help you take the pen apart. Then, see if you can find the spring inside.

The spring in this pen is a **compression spring**.

If you look under the seat of a bicycle, you may find some springs. These are **compression springs.** When the bicycle wheels go over rocks or stones in the road, the **force** of hitting the stones is used to squeeze together the springs. Because the force has been used to squeeze the spring, there is not much force left to reach the person sitting on the seat.

The springs under this bicycle seat mean you get a more comfortable ride.

Cars, bicycles, and buses all use some kind of spring. These springs are called **suspension springs.** Suspension springs **absorb** bumps in the road. Without springs in vehicles, you would feel every stone and dip in the road. Your journey could be very painful!

Did you know that springs are used in cars to make your journey more comfortable?

Bouncing with Springs

A trampoline uses lots of strong **expansion springs.**
The springs join the edge of the trampoline **material** to
the side of the trampoline frame. When you bounce, your
weight pushes down on the middle of the material.
This makes the springs stretch out. All of the springs
then want to go back into shape. They start to pull the
material back up with them, and this makes you lift up
and bounce higher!

Without
springs, bouncing
on a trampoline would
not be much fun!

Pogo stick

A pogo stick is a toy with a spring that you can bounce on for fun. A pogo stick has a very strong **compression spring.** As you bounce on the stick, your weight pushes the **coils** of the spring together. The spring stores this **energy** and then pushes back into its original shape. As the spring stretches back, it pushes the pogo stick upward so that you can bounce up high.

You need good balance to bounce on a pogo stick.

Interesting Springs

Some springs do surprising things. With a long **expansion spring,** you can make a spring walk down stairs!

To get the spring going, it needs to be stretched out.

The spring now wants to pull itself back together again, so it tries to make itself shorter and pulls the back end toward the front.

The **force** of **gravity** pulls the back end of the spring downward until it hits the step below. This happens again and again until the spring has reached the bottom of the stairs.

Springs to measure things

A spring can be made longer by pulling on it using a force. The distance that a spring will stretch is linked to how much force you use to pull it. This means that we can use springs to measure forces and weights. A big force or a heavy weight will make a spring stretch a long way.

The spring in this balance is hidden behind a plastic case. The block is not very heavy, so the spring does not stretch very far.

Springs and Levers

Clothespins are **compound machines.** They use two **levers** and a spring.

Springs in clothespins help them to grip tightly onto objects.

spring

levers

jaws

At each end of the spring, a small piece of metal sticks out straight. These straight parts are stuck to long pieces of wood or plastic, which act as levers. The levers help you push the spring tighter together than it wants to be. This opens the jaws of the clothespin. When you let go, the spring pushes back and closes the jaws on to whatever you want it to grasp.

Hair clips

Some hair clips use springs in the same way as clothespins. They have "teeth" that fit together to hold your hair in place. When you press the top of the hair clip, the spring is pushed tightly together and the teeth open up. The spring does not like to be tight, so it pushes back and makes the teeth close.

The springs in the hair clip push against the teeth to hold your hair in place.

teeth

spring

Sitting on Springs

Every day, people sit and sleep on lots of springs! Inside sofas, underneath the cushions, there are lots of hidden metal springs that help support your body. These are **compression springs.** When you sit on a sofa, you push down on the springs. The springs try to push back to the shape they were before. The pushing of the springs gives support so that you do not sink down into the middle of the sofa.

Springs make your sofa nice and comfortable.

A mattress is the part of your bed that you lie down on. Inside a mattress, there are springs held in a frame. They are squeezed together a little and push against the mattress **material.** The mattress frame helps to spread out the **force** of each spring so that you cannot feel them pushing against you.

mattress frame

springs

mattress material

What would happen without . . . ?

If mattresses were just filled with soft material, or foam, they would soon get squeezed out of shape. Because the springs push back against the material, they give support, and the mattress keeps its shape.

Wind It Up

Old clocks and watches use springs to keep time. A clock is a **compound machine.** It has lots of **simple machines** inside it as well as a special type of spring. The springs used in clocks are called clock springs.

Gear: These turn the fast movement from the spring into slower movement to turn the hands of the clock

Key: This turns the spring

Cog: This is a wheel with "teeth" that turns around. The teeth push against the teeth of other cogs to make them turn, too.

Clock spring: This stores energy

There are lots of different machines inside this alarm clock.

A special key goes into the middle of the clock spring. When the key turns, it tightens the clock spring. The spring stores this **energy** inside the clock. The spring wants to move back to its usual shape. As the spring unwinds, the clock uses **gears** to slow down the movement. Then, the hands of the clock move at the right speed, and the clock starts ticking.

This clock needs to have energy put into it by a person winding up the spring.

Find Out for Yourself

You can find out about springs by talking to your teacher or parents. Think about the **simple machines** you use every day. How do you think they work? Your local library will have books and information about this. You will find the answers to many of your questions in this book, but you can also use other books and the Internet.

Books to read

Fowler, Allan. *Simple Machines*. Danbury, Conn.: Scholastic Library Publishing, 2002.

Glover, David. *What Do Springs Do?* Chicago, ill.: Heinemann Library, 2001.

Using the Internet

Explore the Internet to find out more about springs. Try using a search engine such as www.yahooligans.com or www.internet4kids.com, and type in keywords such as "spring," **"coil,"** and **"lever."**

Glossary

absorb take in

coil length of material wound in circles or rings

compound machine machine that uses two or more simple machines

compression spring spring that is used by squeezing it together

cylinder solid shape with straight sides and a rounded end. Soda cans and toilet paper rolls are shaped like cylinders.

energy power to make things work

expansion spring spring that is used by stretching it out

force push or pull used to move things

gears wheels with teeth (cogs) working together to change the direction or speed of movement

gravity force in nature that pulls everything toward the ground

lever stiff bar or stick that moves around a fixed point

material substance that can be used to make things. Wood, brick, plastic, and paper are all examples of materials.

particles tiny pieces that all materials are made up of

simple machine something that can change the effort force (push or pull you provide) needed to move something or change the direction it moves

stiff something that does not bend easily

suspension spring spring in vehicles such as cars that takes in bumps in the road so that you can have a smooth ride